Jacko Joins the Circus

Written and illustrated
by
Sarah Elizabeth Ashby

First written in 2012....
Some dreams take time, belief and a sprinkle of magic

Dedicated to
my beautiful daughter Scarlett...
and never forgetting Jacko

Published by Black Cat Tales Publishing

First edition 2016

With thanks always and for everything
BB

Text and Illustrations Copyright © Sarah Elizabeth Ashby 2016

All rights reserved.

No part of this publication may be reproduced, stored in or introduced into a retrieval system, or transmitted in any form, or by any means (electronic, mechanical, photocopying, recording or otherwise) without the prior written permission of the author. Any person who does any unauthorised act in relation to this publication may be liable to criminal prosecution and civil claims for damages.

ISBN: 978-0-9955325-0-2

Jacko was my pet dog when I was growing up and we had many adventures together.
The Jacko books are written in his memory
to continue the laughter and joy that he brought.
Also included are many other pals of Jacko.
Can you spot Dot the mouse?

Jacko is a mischievous pup

in a very lovable way

the day he saw the circus in town

he couldn't keep his excitement at bay

He waited for his moment

he waited for his chance

to run off and join the circus

to perform, skip and dance!

Jacko ran down the path
Jacko ran across the green
his barking with excitement
really caused a scene!

Jacko was very excited
howling with delight
but not everyone saw his happiness
Some ran away in fright!

In the tent
the audience was a silent hushhh...
as the elephants balanced ballet
the Super Dog Team interrupted the scene
and mayhem was soon underway!

Mr MacGoo didn't know what to do
chaos hit like a tidal wave!
Fifi slipped
and had a close shave!

'What are you talking about?' huffed Horace The Magnificent horse

'The hot dogs'

'The hot dogs'

'The hot dogs, of course!'

Horace The Magnificent
halted his pace
just as a smile
crept across his face
'SMACK'
eyes wide in surprise
he was hit in the face
with a large custard pie!

The monkeys
had found the candy floss
the doughnuts, the liquorice and party pops
they pinched the clowns' noses
and squeezed squirty posies
whilst tying themselves in knots

Jacko's owner soon recognised him
through the jumble of monkeys, barking and din
with humble apologies and sorries abound
she waded across the panicking crowd

'The hot dogs!
The hot dogs!
We can't leave them here!'

Horace The Magnificent whispered in Jacko's ear
'The hot dogs are just sausages
my old chap
nothing to get into such a flap!'

But!
That's not all from this puppy's tale
when something is wished from the heart
dreams come true...... for dogs, too
and Jacko got to play his part

Not in a circus
and not as a clown
Jacko had become famous all over town!
He had his own show at the local school
'Jacko and the Super Dog Team'
were now very cool!

Some people call them......

'The Cool Dogs'   'The Cool Dogs'   'The Cool Dogs'

Of course!

Especially Horace
The Magnificent horse

Where will Jacko's dreams lead him next........

www.ingramcontent.com/pod-product-compliance
Lightning Source LLC
Chambersburg PA
CBHW061933290426
44113CB00024B/2893